Romances

Romances

poems

LISA AMPLEMAN

LOUISIANA STATE UNIVERSITY PRESS

BATON ROUGE

Published by Louisiana State University Press
Copyright © 2020 by Lisa Ampleman

All rights reserved
Manufactured in the United States of America
First printing

Designer: Barbara Neely Bourgoyne
Typeface: Fournier MT Pro
Printer and binder: LSI

Library of Congress Cataloging-in-Publication Data

Names: Ampleman, Lisa, 1979– author.
Title: Romances : poems / Lisa Ampleman.
Description: Baton Rouge : Louisiana State University Press, [2020]
Identifiers: LCCN 2019036544 (print) | LCCN 2019036545 (ebook) | ISBN 978-0-8071-7119-6 (paperback ; alk. paper) | ISBN 978-0-8071-7306-0 (pdf) | ISBN 978-0-8071-7307-7 (epub)
Subjects: LCGFT: Poetry.
Classification: LCC PS3601.M73 R66 2020 (print) | LCC PS3601.M73 (ebook) | DDC 811/.6—dc23
LC record available at https://lccn.loc.gov/2019036544
LC ebook record available at https://lccn.loc.gov/2019036545

The paper in this book meets the guidelines for permanence and durability of the Committee on Production Guidelines for Book Longevity of the Council on Library Resources. ∞

CONTENTS

I. READING A ROMANCE TOGETHER 1

Preface 3
The Rules of Courtly Love (Abridged, Rev. Ed.) 4
Knight Errant 5
Paul and Fran 6
Love-Scrawls 7
Gemma Donati in Purgatory 8
Gemma Donati, Doppiatrice 9
Laura 10
Anne 13
Dear Lyric Address, 14

II. THE TOXIC UNREQUITED SUITE 15

Him and Me 17
Lady Pygmalion 18
Bedtime Trobairitz 20
My Weak Constitution 21
Jealousy, Inc. 22
Pyrite (He Responds) 23
Dead Ringer 24
Eyeing a New Man 25

III. COURTLY LOVE (FOR COURTNEY LOVE) 27

IV. DRAGONFLY LOVE 51

Felicity, OH 53
Fidelity, MO 54
Victory, WI 55
Pared 56
Eurydice in the ICU Waiting Room 58
Kant the Nephrologist 59
Gilding the Lily 61
Needlework 62

V. THE UNIMAGINED AFTERWARD 63

Courtship 65
Vows 68
Reading *Don Quixote* on Our Honeymoon 69
Espoused 71
Impractical Part 74
Stalwart 75
Watching the Operation 77
The Story's End 79

NOTES 81
ACKNOWLEDGMENTS 85

I

READING A ROMANCE TOGETHER

Preface

after Andreas Capellanus

Dear Walter, I've heard you're a new recruit to Love's defensive line—nose tackle or end, I can't remember—and because I care about your ligaments and bones, I'm sending this message through word of mouth, tweets, status updates, and these frail poems, to share the playbook: how to maintain a continual buzz on Love, or how those with Venus's burrs in their leg hair can untangle themselves. You blogged that you were blocked and knocked down by Love in a scrimmage and lie concussed, unable to drive or make decisions, that doctors have found no cure, and the ruling on the field stands. I can't emphasize how serious this is, in 250 words or 280 characters. I know from experience that someone wearing Love's uniform can think of nothing but how to stay on varsity, the lady barking commands on the sidelines. You think you have nothing worthwhile but what pleases her: brawn and light feet. Therefore, although it's not efficient to sing the same fight song again and again, nor fitting for a healthy young man to endanger his cranium, nevertheless, because of the crush I once had on you, I can't say no. After you know more, you'll be a model citizen: obey speed limits in work zones, use condoms, watch out for girls with spray tans and four-inch heels. Insofar as I can, I'll comply with your desire to know: Here is the art, these are the rules.

The Rules of Courtly Love (Abridged, Rev. Ed.)

after Andreas Capellanus

1. You may love only in autumn, when
   the grapevines brown, and the graves
   along the fence line disappear
   under leaf mounds.

2. Unrequited love is like insulation—toxic
   cotton candy hidden beneath gypsum board.
   It will keep you warm all winter.

3. Marriage is no real excuse for not loving—
   that person wearing your ring is not
   the harridan you imagine, and the years together
   accumulate like rings inside a tree.

4. It is not proper to love the letter carrier
   simply because s/he brings you checks and correspondence.

5. A man in love is a platypus, venomous and growling.

6. A true lover is constantly and without intermission
   possessed by the ghost of Elvis Presley,
   circa 1973, *Aloha from Hawaii*.

7. Nothing forbids a cross-country trip—
   with hitchhiking, Hostess-donette breakfasts,
   and sore feet—to confess your love.

8. Nothing forbids the answer of *no*.

Knight Errant

Call me Night-Error, evening trawler
with a quest and a question. I have undergone
six ordeals, clad in chain mail and spandex:
scaled tenement walls to find a beehive
between bricks—*Apis mellifera*, tremble-dancing
to distribute nectar—and smoked them out;
made it snow in late August, dusting
the old-granny zinnias; hauled off
the harbor rocks so speedboats had safe passage
(*o my frail craft, yawing in the combers*);
lay down on a mattress teeming
with bedbugs and lice, and plucked
single hairs from my scalp for five hours;
ate the red chilis drying on the neighbor's
wooden garden frame; and pulled my friend
from the brink of perilous, cliff-diving love
(if one can ever pull another from the brink).
I brought these merit badges documenting
the feats to lay at your feet, o demanding one
(*dies irae, dies illa, quantus tremor est futurus*).
I wrote my tale out in cursive and gave an illuminator
fifty bucks to add gold-leaf letter-animals
in the margins and sprinkle it with rose water.
Hearken, lend an ear in this crepuscular hour:
I seek respite. Your hand on the small of my back.
Will you read? Will you bemadam me?

Paul and Fran

*Noi leggiavamo un giorno per diletto
di Lancialotto come amor lo strinse . . .*

We were reading one day for pleasure
of Lancelot and how love felled him . . .
　　—*Inferno,* Canto V

Reading a romance novel together
was the kindling, though they'd intended
to mock it, the stiffening members
and softening flesh. The hero tripped
and fell onto the couch, trapping
the sassy but stubborn lass under his
broad shoulders and muscled
chest. *I burn for you,* he said. And when
he kissed his woman, Paul did too,
though Fran was engaged to his brother.
Paperback tossed to the floor, they canoodled
on the futon. When Johnny heard, he bound them
together in the trunk and set the Chevy on fire.

But *romance* also means language,
so let's give them a reprieve, start the story
over. Paul reads Fran the dictionary instead.
They're on the pronunciation
guide. \ü\ as in *bou*doir, \ä\ as in *lin*gerie.
She doesn't understand he's making a pass.
A couch dumped in front of her apartment
smolders, flame-resistant material
refusing to combust. It will lie
out there, growing soggy with rain,
until the sanitation department
comes to haul it away.

Love-Scrawls

We carve trees, scrape the bark to make our confession,
our affinities simplified to initials
in a lopsided heart. We mark bathroom stalls
in rest stops, black Sharpie and ballpoint pen,

safety pin: BL loves Dusty '89. Jared and Mary-Ann.
Some of us carry our hearts
on our biceps—or half a heart,
with the missing part tattooed on the beloved's arm.

Flesh stretches, ink fades.
A laser can burn off the evidence
if Mary-Ann moves to Milwaukee. Trees mend
themselves—that black walnut struck

by a panel truck slowly covered up its wound
over twenty years, leaving only a small hollow
near the ground. After all, who did you love
when you were fifteen?

Gemma Donati in Purgatory

Gemma stayed home when Dante
had to leave. She did not
miss him, as far as we know,
did not grieve the loss of the man
down the hall, composing poems
not for her. He traveled for years
alone. Then, perhaps, she joined him
in Ravenna. Then, perhaps,
they reconciled. Or grinned
with closed jaws for the sake
of the kids. Easy to ignore
the rumors about her temper,
the meddlers exalting a fable
about a girl dead and buried
long ago. Sure, her name
does not mean *blessed*.
But what if she's in the poem,
la gemma, the ring on a corpse's finger:
La Pia, murdered by her husband.
Every time he wrote *la donna*,
he erased her from the record.
A jewel signifies a contract,
carefully arranged.
A ring can seal a letter
not meant for others' eyes.

Gemma Donati, Doppiatrice

She works alone,
or so it seems, the dark room
with hanging mike and headphones

a sensory-deprivation chamber.
She repeats the lines again and again
to get the timing right. Not the muse,

nor the singer, she says someone else's
words. When the blonde teen speaks
in any movie, Gemma is her voice,

italiana, all those vowels wrong
for how that mouth moves,
but the ice-lined tone just right.

She speaks for her, ventriloquist,
when she acts on television too.
Cruel when she needs to be, when Ashley is,

she can steal a boy or scene.
When the red light turns off,
she is not in a hotel, nor high school,

no garish sets waiting to be made real.
She's a brunette, in fact,
can have dinner in a piazza

while *le ragazze* giggle in groups.
They would know her voice,
if she spoke, but not her face.

Laura

Mother, honest Lucretia did it best.
She had an iron spine and quick dagger
and knew: without honor, there's no lady,
no life. He gave me a pet name and let me speak
briefly, but only after death. Avignon
has too many corpses moldering.
Unlike them, I became eternal, though
first my fingers turned black, and boils
roiled under my skin. I sported black freckles.
Now, in séance, he summons my voice.
"I only wait for you," he makes me say.
"My lovely veil." My lovely squirrel-fur cloak
and green kirtle. "Peace be with you.
We will meet again." My mouth speaks
less than my eyes, his light-friends,
which tell him he needs to let sorrow go.
The knot of his life, sweaty gnarled tassel,
needs to become gray, not untangle.
Francesco, I am cruel to you for *good*.
Sigh no more, sir. Here's a palm
for victory and a laurel for triumph.
A naked spirit, I am not what you dreamed.
Here's my missing gangrenous limb,
exposed to the air. Here's my pale belly.
Your beloved has been dust for decades
(but before, vomited blood, skin burning).
My final speech: "It is pleasing to hear
your arguments, but I need more time
to consider your case." And, concerned
with salvation, he turns to Mary instead.
All a woman has is her honor.

Talor risponde e talor non fa motto

("Sometimes she responds, and sometimes she can't make a reply")
—Petrarch, Poem 336

Mother
    an iron spine
        without honor   no lady
                          let me speak
      after death
        corpses moldering

                    black freckles
Now, in séance
I   wait for you
        My lovely
            Peace be with you
We will meet again

            let
The knot of his life
                be untangled
Francesco,
Sigh
        a laurel for triumph
  naked   I am
      missing
        air
Your beloved   for decades
          blood   burning
      It is pleasing to hear

> your   need
>   consider
>   salvation
>   a woman

Anne

No one may touch me. In the empty cages
                of church choirs. In the nebulous woods.
In Caesar's preserve or the back chamber

                of a lady's room at court. But admire
the whiteness of my face swimming on the canvas's
                      black. Once, walking in Greenwich,

    we came across the sunken dark soil
            where a tree, roots and all,
    had been removed. Wild violets

                    repopulated the site.
A deer with wasting disease walks the same path
            repetitively, shies from others of its kind,

    lowers its head, listless. Let it crash
through the underbrush on its circuit,
                and do not graze

    its matted fur. The stricken doe
smells already like rotten meat;
            do not put yourself in her danger.

Dear Lyric Address,

you're my default. I like to ride
in your wake. I'm that girl
on roller skates, holding on
to your bicycle seat. There

are my tracks in the snow,
four meager lines following
as far as they can.
I'm shivering. Your eyes

are on the sidewalk ahead,
the curb where you might
bounce me off. Wait. Wait.
I can yodel *you who*

with the best of them.
I don't care who listens in,
pretending they're you
holding the handlebars

so tight your knuckles
whiten. Or pretending
they're me, ankles sore
from keeping my balance,

mouth going dry
(tongue a dumb tool)
from speaking to you
and speaking to you.

II

THE TOXIC
UNREQUITED SUITE

Him and Me

after Gaspara Stampa, Poem 7

You ladies who want to know my guy,
visualize a man of wandering grace, sweet-cheeks,
young in years but sage as an elderly owl,
a paragon of glory and valor, blond as a bat,
flushed from the cold, a tall man with oak-barrel
torso, a perfect opera when the baritone
gets the girl. Except (alas, a lapse)
a little impish in love.

And whoever wants to see me, suppose
a woman in every semblance the image of death
and martyrdom, wearing billowing black trash bags—
but also a hotel for sturdy, work-a-day faith.
One who cries, torrifies, and sighs
but can't make her lover more merciful.

Lady Pygmalion

I made you in my image, curio,
old-fashioned unsmiling face
inside a ring of seashells,
something to gaze at when I got lonely

or the sunset was bland. You were
barnacle covered and moss laden
but smelled so sweet, the sea gone bad
and then good. Not fish,

but coconut-slathered skin in sun,
plus salt. Your hat never shaded your face
quite right. I remade you, three
dimensions, colored in the cheekbones

and did a spot-check. Your facial features
mimicked mine, the ratio of nose line
to eye socket. Your torso archaic
when I took down the head

to shine the eyeballs, which went dull
with dust every month. Only paste and oats
behind them. You were agreeable.
When you vanished, the mirror said

I was a sack tied loosely to a stake,
sleeves coming apart at the seams,
straw ripe for bird beaks.
Their precarious nests in the eaves,

a single abandoned blue egg. A bird
on the sidewalk that seemed injured

but flew away fine. I don't need
to know what kind it was (pigeon? dove?)

when it's gone anyway. Small orb
wrapped in tinsel and tape,
little creature inside scratching
something I can't understand.

Bedtime Trobairitz

I'm tempted to pull tight the floss
caught between molars and pluck it
like a lute, but then I could not also sing,

and you deserve more than dull strumming
and would only roll your eyes.
How wonderful that in plainchant

the voices hold the note
no matter how long the words take
until the next tone descends

on a string from the ceiling.
You can sing anything to the same tune.
Cowled monks in one voice: O blessed

virgin Mary. Jongleur strumming:
my heart, dart-shot, your archer eyes.
Plunk, plunk. It doesn't matter:

You've gone to bed early;
the hallway light besmearing your face
is no sun, and this is no alba.

My Weak Constitution

> My love is as a fever, longing still
> For that which longer nurseth the disease.
> —Shakespeare, Sonnet 147

You're the hectic in my blood,
the bacteria on my spoon,
the heated remnants of my appendix
curdling in my gut. But I despise

you. I ferret you out and lick
the bottom of your shoes—morsel
of a leaf, soil, salty rain—spit shine them
clean. Like a raccoon

on trash night, with his little
people-hands, you can rummage
through my cans unimpeded.
I'll take the antitoxin, bubble-gum

flavored, and sweat you out
the next time, or the next.

Jealousy, Inc.

Her laugh could cut crystal. Her tiny hand is curled
in yours, soft mouse at rest. Her mouth is a cherry stem,
knotted. Oh, my scarecrow, man-not-mine,
she disheartens me. Your birdseed, your treasure,
your marsupial. I would leave the stove on,
let the blue devils dance their gassy mazurka all day;
would incorporate, limit liability; would lash
a sail to my side (weak rowboat tossed by every eddy),
to have your hand in mine. Every poet thinks it's the beloved
who calls forth words, but truly it's terror.
The possible futures forestalled by your coupling,
the countless wasted hours of my ardor. I appraise & cipher.
I tally, I tarry.

Pyrite (He Responds)

You said we struck
sparks, like fool's gold
and steel, and I wanted
to warn you: I'd never
winked, just a muscle
tic in my eyelid. So
build a pyre for me,
exorcise me in the blue
fever, the high BTUs
where no soot gathers.
You'll be burning
a paper doll you cut
out of foolscap and
decorated yourself.
I admire your potential
for invention, whether
wood stacking or
character development.
I am not the companion
you amalgamated, but
the smirk's a fair copy.
Pyrite, with water,
produces sulfuric acid,
acid rain, it's the spark
behind mine fires,
the defect inside
Chinese drywall that
makes people sick.
You courted roof-fall,
crystal radios, a man
with hands that stain
brown in winter rain.

Dead Ringer

You, a year later,
in a hotel lobby—
no, your double,
trench-coated man
with leonine hair.
My sternum on fire,
the room still
cocktail-hour dim
with small lamps
like embers.
Selfishly, I think:
miss me. See my
shade in one of our
old haunts. She'll see
right through you:
masquerade knight
feigning he's set down
his lance and chest plate.

Eyeing a New Man

after Gaspara Stampa, Poem 206

Love made me live within the flame
of a candle wick, like a salamander newly born,
or like the phoenix, no less strange, who lives
and expires in the same fire.

Feeling pleasure is all that matters. The trick
is to walk over coals and not feel
pain—and not care that he
who led me there feels no pity.

Just as my ardor for him was extinguished
and I finished the firewalk, Love lit a second
inferno, more torrid than the first, for another.

I can't regret this exquisite blaze. I'll twirl
inside it as long as my new beau,
heart-thief, is satisfied with how I burn.

III

COURTLY LOVE

(for Courtney Love)

I. ALL YOU WHO HEAR

I'm a good lady.
I'm a good lay.
I sing a good lay.
Voi che sapete
che cosa è amor.
I'll ache
like the fiancée
tainted. I'll disobey.

Listen to the strum,
to the feedback's guitar-hum,
and though you call me strumpet,
bitch, bleached-blonde itch-
satisfier, I rise. I climb
the charts like a live wire.

II. PRECEPTS

You must have sun-eyes, they said,
and hair to match, a head
full of sunflowers, and a hand-
ful of arrows, self-command,
and voluminous skirts.
You're allowed to flirt
with one and all, provided
you're muse to only one, undivided

attention on the page. Love-child,
be anything but wild,
be mysterious and dull, they chided.
Be coy and refuse—both dessert
and advances. Let go of your firebrand
ways, hold onto your maidenhead.

III. SHE REPLIES

I am my own sun, and peroxide
makes me blond enough, I guess.
Ferocious as Diana, I tried
archery in high-school gym class.

I've got a closet full of mini-
skirts, and I love to flirt, but I write
my own story: better to be skinny
than fat, better to bite

than be bitten. I'm the honey
in your tea, the smitten girl
with more on her mind than money
(nice pecs), the mother-of-pearl

knife in your ribs. My maidenhead?
How about your restraint instead.

IV. FIRST SIGHT

You were a wraith onstage;
Love's archer strung his bow
and socked me in the chest, handcuffed me to the cage
that would be my home. Whoso

list to hunt, I know a worthy prey:
you—your ice-blue eyes, bee-whine voice, honey hair.
But I was senseless, my sunburned brain
as useless as underwear.

Still, fainting I followed. I asked
to see you again—you said yes, then
didn't show. I offered you a flask
of whiskey, a needle (I'm sorry), myself (again).

You spurned me, your arms long and small.
Persistent, I committed to the free fall.

V. THE CLIFF OVER WAIKIKI

You wore pajamas to our wedding—
blue checked—comfortable rara avis,
and after the vows, after the sunset kiss,
we both held pink flowers, shedding
those gender roles we hated.
I did don a gauzy gown, my hair
mussed by the wind. But I didn't care
about being the bride; I waited
for that other bird curled inside me
to be born. In our photos, my face
is solemn; you grin, aleatory prodigy.
We wouldn't celebrate our third anniversary—
I'd read your suicide note with its fucked-up grace,
to our gathered guests: lonely liturgy.

VI. MADONNA

I am like Mary: I hold a Bean
in my arms for pictures. I made her,
mother her, lick her dirty face clean,
wear her in a sling pack. Officer,
you can't take her. My house is pristine,
heroin use only a rumor,
and everything else best kept between
husband and wife. Oh, inquisitor,
the cameras are fickle: they'll tail
you home in your brief flurry of fame:
the one who cuffed Courtney. She's to blame
for endangerment, he's the all-hailed
cop—until Buttafuoco's in jail
and they turn away: bloodhounds, new trail.

VII. BONDAGE

I loved a man as wrong as rain,
as right as red paint,
as strict as whips and chains.
He was my nothingness,
my bodhisattva, my less
self-conscious-in-a-dress.

When I did the math,
we came out equal,
modern-rock miracle
queen of the riffraff.
I was his S, I was his M.
My boy in layered sweaters
had me in velvet fetters
but sang himself a requiem.

VIII. HORSEMAN

You wound me, dear Sir, with your cornflower eyes
and your blond-stringed hair and your two-toned
20-gauge shotgun. You bring me along
when you travel abroad, but that girl Death

finds you, singing, in Rome, gives you pill
after pill, tells you oblivion is better.
That harpy brings you a horse with fierce
gallop, and you suit up with saddle and spurs.

You ride to a greenhouse where the flowers
aren't potted yet and bury your fingers in humus.
And where is my bonny lad, and why aren't I
with him? And where is his steed and dear daughter?

You leave me a note under one flowerpot
to tell me the hell-hag was right.

IX. CURT REPLY

The wind of nirvana greases up my hair.
Freedom from pain, but not follicles, not flakes,
not orange Tang, all the floss & prickly pear
of existence: consciousness in limbo, fake
repentance. We deadpan ghouls have stomachaches.
We pendulum. At the end of every prayer
we sigh *Namu Amida Butsu*, aware
being reborn is dissolving, not a break.

So, I'm the susurration when the wind dies
down, love, the battery acid to mix with
your Evian water (we always tangled
well), stubborn mote lodged, itchy, in the mind's eye.
Sing your elegies, make me paladin, myth:
your lost savior is not angel but angle.

X. WHAT SHALL I DO?

Che debb' io far?
—Petrarch, Poem 268

The worst crime is faking it, he said, and
died. My fatal moon, my gentle combat.
He could medicate with smack, lead a band
in angst, nearly stumble on a hi-hat,
and still kiss his daughter good night. His hands
signed *sorrow-filled*—delicate acrobats—
but it looked like an A-chord. Understand,
he kept secrets, a foreign diplomat.

But I injected him with Narcan to bring
him back before a show. I called the cops
then changed my tune when he unlocked the door.
No one can set me free. O Death, your sting
is nothing. You flatten the mountaintops
in fog, but I croon my solo encore.

INTERLUDE

Oh, Courtney dear, I made you say some things
that aren't true—at best, they're conjectures
I culled from online rumors; oh, the slings
and arrows of the rabid blogosphere,
your hand on the syringe only a pipe
dream to help me explain the loss you felt.
I could as well have said you'd reached to wipe
a tear with one young hand and, shaken, knelt
under the grief. But that's bad writing, Court.
I will disclose I knew your brother (half)—
we shared a class in college on the men
who, deemed Romantic, sighed deeply and wrote
some heady stuff. Your brother was brilliant, deft—
and I sat silent, taking notes—yes, then

as now. I'm slave to books—your mother's, yours—
the Google search, your blog. Without a thought
I could claim as original. Ignore
the flaws; I cannot theorize without
gouging a hollow in attempted wholes.
At heart, I'm an A-minus girl, adept
at masquerade: see, here's my headscarf, kohl,
and rouge, but what you don't see is unkempt
hair and my ragged nails. I'd never brave
the ropeline at a club; you're in the V-
I-P room. Oh, Courtney, perhaps you should
write your own story. I'll try to behave:
refrain from practicing hyperbole,
mythologizing you. Repent. Do good.

XI. HOLE

Girl, sing it like a bore-hole. Headless dolls
like chicken corpses, empty cavity
and floppy toy arms: these fiends caterwaul
in corners, creepy mascots, stage debris,

eerie companions. Their abandoned heads
have Os as mouths, their skulls as hollow as
crack houses. Greedy, desperate, never bled
nor breathed, they imitate you, second-class

performer. They're kinderwhores. Garb yourself
in frilly dresses, wear their vacant look.
Well versed in crafting and carving the self,
you pose like fish bait dangling on a hook.

No matter what you tell yourself, doll heart,
the missing parts make possible the art.

XII. "SEX, DEATH, LOVE, HATE"

Punk pop
Noise rock
Needle stick
Doll smock

Stage dive
Dope high
Celebrity
Oh my

Fast flame
Mary Jane
Dirty Blonde
Cocaine

Twitter feed
Let it bleed

XIII. SETTING THE RECORD STRAIGHT

You know me as a blond chameleon,
from drug addict to haute couture, but what
the headlines leave out are theology
studies in Ireland (Trinity College),
a novelist grandmother I never met,
my recitation of a poem by Plath
the time I tried to join the Mickey Mouse
Club, and devotion to the Buddha's way.

But, true: My mother ditched me when she moved
abroad. My father gave me LSD
when I was four; my mind was freed. I've fought
(or skirmished with) the bête noire of drugs,
and once I stood near windows, almost thought
to jump—what else do you expect from Love?

XIV. DESIRE

I want my face emblazoned on your chests,
my eyes to be the ones you stare into
at night, floating, ghostly, on a poster.
I want to be your fucked-up heroine.

You could be coy and download bootlegged songs;
instead of money, give me compliments,
write me blog posts, retweet my every word.
Venerate me in the glitterati.

But Fame, that fickle whore, entices you
with other starlets, pimping them as sweet
and sexy, songbirds with their brilliant plumage.

And, hardhearted, you let my album languish
in the bargain bin, skip my comeback tour,
and listen to those minxes' chirping trills.

XV. LOVE, THE MODEL; LOVE, THE DESIGNER

The body is a mannequin
waiting to be dressed.
I wear a Dalmatian
coat and tiara embossed
with peace symbols. *Let it bleed*,
my inner arm declares in Gothic script.
The world is a globe, emptied,
before me. My guitar, an airstrip
closed for repair. My own designs
I dub *Never the Bride*,
for the woman who wants to wear
vintage rags made new: refined,
flirtatious. In the dresses' hems I hide
a ruby. Every girl needs a jeweled snare.

XVI. THE ADMIRER SPEAKS

Oh, my glamour-shot queen, your blond tresses
and lingerie-under-sequined-jacket
are just for me, your red swollen lips bless
me with curses, with cast-off cigarette.
I put it with my collection, a set
of guitar picks, fingernails, cassettes:
your band in its early glory, distressed
and drug laden, but equipped for success.

I wait outside your building for the sight
of your rail-thin beauty, mismatched fabrics
and oversized sunglasses. Would you let
me touch your clavicle in the moonlight
or give me the finger, dominatrix?
Let me breathe in your ear: I'm no threat.

XVII. CRUEL LADY

in Frances Bean Cobain's voice

She killed my pets. Not with arsenic
or by drowning them in the bathtub,
but bad enough: my dog found her stash
of sleeping pills, and the cat entangled
itself in trash, sample fabrics, paper work.
She told everyone my dad's friend
made a pass at me. *Him, I am about
to shoot dead,* she said online.

False, of course. There's a reason
I wear my hair dark and tattoo myself
in French: *L'art est la Solution au Chaos*,
not love. I learned to give her tea
while waiting for the ambulance. I learned
not to hold out for affection's dregs.

XVIII. GIVE IT UP

I know how to take off a halter top
with panache, and when I needed money,
I'd find a strip club that would let me drop

my drawers for cash. I'd twine my body
around the pole like ivy, that pesky
creeping weed, let the men call me "bunny"

or "sweetie"—all they want is a fleshy
daydream, a risqué fiction breathing, bare.
But when, at forty (still built and leggy),

I started writing songs again, I swear,
I didn't want a man looking at me,
distracting me. I gave up love, affairs,

even sex. I espoused celibacy;
making music was my ecstasy.

XIX. IF

(in her own words)

We'd probably live on the Upper West Fucking Side now
and have three fucking kids.
We might even have divorced, like,
both be on our third marriage.
He might be a playwright or have his latest show
at MOMA. I'd have a sixteen-year-old son
and be the model wife. Given the money
involved here, we could probably have had
a fucking yacht. I don't fucking know.
If he came back right now,
I'd have to kill him for what he did to us.
I'd fucking kill him.
I'd fuck him,
and then I'd kill him.

XX. APOLOGIA

Dear Courtney, mea culpa, I am sorry
for parroted squawkings and out-and-out lies,
for putting your words in the Lady's mouth
and making her my sock puppet.
I liked the way my hand felt as it jawed
and lisped, how it knew what to say,
gloved like a falconer's forearm.

I transcribe and mimeograph you for the sake
of those who've loved and lost, or sighed
over a sonnet. Or believed in Laura (that
phantom, never flesh). For the women
who never desired in print or song
but were crooning all along into the ears
of carrier pigeons that then flew free.

IV

DRAGONFLY LOVE

Felicity, OH

The brick-and-siding bungalows have sun
crawling up their sides. Oh, the black-eyed
Susans in the ditch. Oh, the empty bag
of Cheetos. There's the house that copper
thieves loved for its rail-thin pipes
and vacant rooms. There, balloons
blossom from the Felicity Arms's sign,
as if to say, *Live here, there's an empty pool
still redolent of chlorine*. Two bus-stop kids
wait in egg-yolk light, one longing to have
a balloon, even if it sags to the ground,
the other pulling at a sweater string—how
long could it be? Oh, the places they'll go.
Oh, the places we'll leave. A telephone pole
gathers teddy bears and wreaths to itself.
Just down 222, a recent wreck settles in the road,
cars at odd angles. The drivers have not yet
opened their doors, but it's possible to
fix a dislodged bumper, replace a broken
brake light. Someone will sweep up
the shards, someone else direct traffic
onto the shoulder. A line of cars waits
patiently to clear the mess, even
as traffic backs up past the parking lot
of the Mini Mart. Inside, from her
high perch, a three-year-old
in her foam-green swimsuit hurls
cereal boxes into the cart. Oh, the fiber
and bran, sugar and oats. Oh, her toothy grin
since her mother hasn't noticed
and the candy aisle is next.

Fidelity, MO

The only wind here is the distant whirr
of highway. In its warren, a rabbit reflexively

pulls out fur to cradle its bloody-thumb
babies. The woodstove in that ranch house

wafts the scent of pine down the cul-de-sac.
A flag, not lowered in three years, is thin

as linen and pinned by one corner
to a poplar branch. On the porch,

a woman smokes while she waits for the car.
And there's the Pontiac, a red fox,

blazing through the trees.
There's his mug-face through the rain

as he walks up, still singing
that classic-rock hymn: *forever*

yours, faithfully. His scarf askew,
his smile a half-moon on its back.

Today's a ragtime ditty, half-speed.
She's off to the diner for the lunch rush,

and he'll sleep. Today's a fried-egg sandwich,
bottomless cup of coffee, cottoned sleep,

as the late-day western sun
cuts a cloudbank into a slab of beef.

Victory, WI

All hail the crumbling stone monument
to the Battle of Bad Axe, the wooden helve

long rotted and burned, the short walk to the river,
where we can bathe in its brown,

where a steamboat-ghost huffs out
a stream of bullets. We are invulnerable

to their spectral lead, descendants
of fur traders (beaver, ermine,

skunk). Our lungs are clean and pink. Let's visit
the saw shop, the greenhouse with bluff views,

the pines and stacks of firewood,
the Blackhawk general store, named for

the warrior who waved a chalky,
misunderstood flag and eluded capture

for weeks. In winter, eagles
dive here, gathering lift when the wind

hits the bluffs: all hail the migrating
raptor, its piercing talon and yellow cere.

Pared

Ghost ship, the partly
        dismantled Ferris wheel
                pulses in the wind,

half still anchored
        to the axle. They've
                removed the rest,

one pie-slice section
        at a time. The former
                wonder—decorated O

garish with citrine
        lights—is now mostly
                folded into

compressed hinges
        on a flatbed. Claudia, you
                rode the mortal circuit

of such a wheel
        in a final poem,
                raised up, swung down.

A body held
        in the beloved's arms
                like a Pietá, pity,

straining the shoulder
        and elbow joint.
                They couldn't

blast away
    the first Ferris wheel's
        axle, buried it

(twenty-six stories long)
    near the fairgrounds.
        Every few decades

we try to suss it out
    with sonar or shovels.
        I know that your

pen would prune
    for me these lines
        that mimic the shape

of yours, would remove
    yourself, leave
        just the half-circle

simulating a boat,
    moored in the wrong
        place, ferrying no one.

Eurydice in the ICU Waiting Room

This time he was the one who tried to slip
under, no viper fanged with poison,
no coterie of sharp-handed women,
but vertigo, a headache, brain unzipped
by a bleed. Winter sidewalks go slick
in spots from underground heat, sewer breath,
that inconsequential god of death
holding a fiddle he can't play. Just blink:
your love is here, girded with tubes and wires.
Men with their small saws opened his skull,
relieved the pressure with a shunt. He will—
with shaved head and paralyzed voice box—require
a wheelchair, a walker, but come back to you,
this enthrallment just another limbo to pass through.

Kant the Nephrologist

Transplanted from Königsberg, our Immanuel—
active, rational subject—evaluates kidneys.

He finds them disinterestedly beautiful:
the branching grace of the renal artery,

cortex nestled around the salty medulla,
U-shaped loop of Henle aiding the filtration.

Remarkable, too, the tubing that can sift
the body's blood through an arm vein

when the kidneys—poisoned by sugar,
alcohol, disease—cannot, and the categorical

imperative of the transplant-list protocol.
On his daily constitutional past Starbucks,

he considers the amount of caffeine
one must ingest before calcium stones

form. If the patient's flank radiates
pain and the urine is cloudy or burns,

Dr. Kant can set him (or her) straight
with extracorporeal shock waves.

He's never married, enjoys red wine
in moderation. Doesn't complain

when the office clerk tells a patient
"we pronounce it *cant*."

He sees the thing-in-itself
in films shot through a patient's skin—

ultrasound, CT scan, the sublimity of organs
suspended in darkness, aurora borealis—

and in his hands: the pocked surface
of a removed polycystic, or the glistening,

palm-sized gift from a relative or stranger,
one quarter-pound of goodwill.

Gilding the Lily

To keep anxiety at bay, my friend called chemo *dragonfly love*. Those insects—christened, in places, *the devil's darning needles*—hover as they contort their joined bodies into a heart, the male with pincers. Finger cutter, horse killer, ear stick, eye pisser. *Look closely at the eyes of a female darner and you may well see dark puncture marks.* As a slow drip through an IV. As a pill. Through a port into a vein. She called nausea *erotica*. Just the same, we name our storms to lessen them—not a tropical cyclone, but *Arabella*, with ballet shoes and bun. Tumors, too, were *friends*, waiting at the bus stop with backpacks in the morning. Cindy French braids Carrie's hair, yanking at the scalp to form the tight crisscross. Not hair loss, but *deep conditioning*. She gave us the new lexicon on stationery embossed with a red rose speckled by raindrops. The stem still had its thorns. Ring-around-the-rosy, red rover, red rover, send her right over. She called death *the world of 10,000 things:* the dragon courting its damsel, catheter tubing in the waste bin, video of a toddler biting his brother, pas de deux, full-sugar ice cream, Crimson Queen, Trumpeter, Red Knockout, Tuscany Superb . . . I knew her as Rose Shapiro. At the funeral I learned she was born *Passalacqua:* to cross the river, to pass a glass of water.

Needlework

All those tapestry faces
singing or yawning,
eyes closed, heads uplifted
to whatever light
the thread implies.
Their feet fray.
Their hands have no fingers.
They are praising their God,
or bored, in unison.
I want to put my finger,
its knitted whorls,
on the one whose chest
is ripping open,
the knot tugged,
the way a fingernail,
weak, pulls on fabric
to the point where
it's breaking
but does not break.

V

THE UNIMAGINED AFTERWARD

Courtship

(a canzone)

In order to participate in my first
      kiss, I rode to the fairgrounds
in a crowded back seat on someone's lap, found
his hand as we walked past the ring toss, concert
      pavilion, funnel-cake stand.
The wheel stood, blinking, past them. A sweaty man
opened the little gate for us. Inexpert
in the sacred rituals of *going out*,
I sat immobile, his arm behind me, hand
on my shoulder. And when the wheel's movement stopped,
      we were rocking on the top,
suspended above the carnival. He leaned
      over, easy mouth, no tongue.
I thought I should have been kissed before fourteen
but here it was: Ferris wheel, evening, Chris Young.

But then, years of admiring at a distance,
seeing courtship in any kindness: sideways
glance meant undying devotion; the mildest praise
      could have been a veiled advance.
I invented suitors, the silly inverse
of Penelope, unweaving my own hurt.
I blame Mr. Darcy, who withholds romance
      until the novel's end, plays
      the bachelor, reserved, terse.
Of course, all along, he loved her, and every
amorous feeling was held in secrecy.
So, I too was a naïve heroine sniffing out
signs, waiting for a declaration. Even
indifference could be love to a devout
believer—a simple fondness could deepen.

Jaded, newly a doubter, though, when I met
you, I did not expect you to look at me
      when you said something funny,
to ask for my number. And I, no coquette,
got yours too. Still, when you invited me to
a high-school musical, I had to redo
      my internal tape-cassette
that played only sad songs in a minor key;
yes, no games, no ploys. I was being pursued.
Your students sang, "I don't know how to love him,"
and one was Jesus Christ. When the lights went dim
after intermission, you leaned in and asked
if I wanted to get a drink afterward.
      "Oh sure," I whispered and grasped
your hand, surprised you. Overeager lovebird.

Then, more conventional courting: twinkling lights
at the nighttime zoo, gloved hand holding gloved hand;
dinner, chicken marsala (a man who can
      cook!); sweet lip-to-lip good nights;
      You opened up my car door,
sat with me in the hospital as I swore
through the pain of appendicitis. White knight,
      honey pie, chivalrous man,
you asked me to join you at a jewelry store.
      See, I didn't know a thing
about cut, carat, color, clarity, rings,
or bands. I wore a few and then let you pick.
No surprise then when you read a poem, proposed
at what would be our dinner table, a wick
dancing with flame, a vase with a single rose.

Now, our home sits empty while we're out at night
    (low-key dinner, late movie),
framed wedding moments, dull clutter, potpourri.
The dirty dishes in the sink are all right—
    I'll clean them in the morning.
The newspapers on the chair for recycling,
the crushed soda cans in a bin don't invite
romance in the same way. No catastrophe:
we still have pet names, honey, the songs I sing
to you on a whim, the simple serenade
of a basement cricket. Having overstayed
    his welcome, he chirps his tune
to sweaters drying on a rack, my childhood
books, laundry, the packed-up Christmas tree. He croons,
bachelor in the sump pump, misunderstood.

    To his desperate trill, I'll add this little song,
    form stolen from Petrarch, a rhetoric not
    my own, medieval prosody we forgot.

Vows

an epithalamium

You hauled me out of bed,
all wires and tubes,

too weak to stand.
Walked with me

when I moved so
slowly you joked

we were going backward.
It was no repayment

when I helped you sling
your broken elbow,

your arm curled, wing,
in front of your body.

There's no ledger, no balance;
we can't speed the collagen

hardening into new bone.
I can open the blinds

before you arrive home,
give you words

(this earnest thing),
vow to walk with you,

forward or backward,
over black ice, hospital tile, fire.

Reading *Don Quixote* on Our Honeymoon

Dulcinea does not (cannot) read. But I do,
beachside in a brown two-piece,

at ease in Cancun. The carmine cover,
though, is embarrassing, gleaming helmet

with gorget to protect the neck.
You layered lotion on yours

because even the morning sun
is relentless. We've stolen a reserved

but unoccupied haven under a thatch palapa,
the other couple downing slushy drinks

at the clear chlorinated pool
—or they're ensconced in

the stone-floored, cool rooms
we all retreat to. The ocean

is azure, the sky cerulean,
the sand white—all performing their roles

with gusto. But I perspire,
like some medieval woman

winnowing wheat. My hair is ridiculous,
waves amplified by humidity.

And after an oceanfront massage,
I feel only faint and dehydrated.

Captivity is the greatest evil
that can befall men, the book's man

tells his friend, and here you are,
yoked to me, who wants to sit alone

for twenty minutes, send you to the ATM
on your own, return to the woebegone knight.

The beloved in literature is a construct;
the one next to you in paradise

has the vinyl lounge chair
stuck to her back with sweat.

Espoused

I.

Ice chunks fallen to the road
from tractor-trailer roofs are gray matted roadkill,

curled in on themselves.
We haven't spoken since Terre Haute,

scrubby deciduous trees
all the same beige. The quibble itself

doesn't matter. I ice
my insides, run my necklace's charm

on its chain with a free hand to feel
the twang while I drive. You (tiny fighter, tiny guns),

playing games on your phone,
battle, die, and wait to resurrect on a small screen.

Your game map shows
the path home, but first, the rapids and cannibals.

II.

The river carries me, but my heart
remains with you, he sang in the pub

last night, the banjo player
whose shirt praised the men who weld and solder.

He wore a metal half-circle
around his neck—no fetter. When he turned,

I saw two steel pieces
braced on his clavicle, and the harmonica

they held, which he turned
into mournful wheezing. When he wasn't breathing

into it, he sang of a steamboat fire,
the craft an evening candle for riverside homes

as it floated away.
I touched your pant leg

with my foot, so lightly
it might have been accidental.

The thing is, the music shifted then,
rollicked, the stand-up bass

a dancer who'd surprised himself with movement.
One fan, caught up,

percussed the table with his hand and wedding ring,
its weight a golden snare

marking the backbeat, ally to the band
who had no drummer.

III.

At the next truck stop, you'll buy
a large Coke and take over, driving us

into the somber hills of southern Indiana,
though the late sun will enamel them.

Radio voices telling us stories will lull me
to sleep, the car a rocking chair,

the pavement a steady bass line, and I'll
wake when you touch my knee—almost idly,

out of deep habit—and ask if I'm
ready to stop for dinner together.

Impractical Part

> As for you, my galvanized friend, you want a heart. You don't know how lucky you are not to have one. Hearts will never be practical until they can be made unbreakable.
> —*The Wizard of Oz*

I know a man whose heart is not his own,
who at thirty slowly became statuary,
gray stranger, until that lump of muscle
from another was rib-spread, vein-sewn,
paddle-shocked into his chest. Common
miracle. The meds to keep his system
from objecting to this fortunate,
strange piece move through his kidneys,
which, over ten years, will tire of the chore.

In Boccaccio, women salt their dead lovers'
hearts with their tears, carry them in golden cups.
Guillaume's wife eats the organ, unknowing.
Ghismonda pours poison over it and drinks.
It's all the same: ache, attack, murmur, failure.
A yogi believes in red lotus blossoms unfurling.
In pictures, Jesus exposes his Sacred Heart,
the cloak of his body turned inside out
to show the stitching: a flaming pomegranate,
braceleted by thorns.

Since he was sewn together, my friend has helped
make two children—two aortas, two tricuspid valves,
all the wrench-and-socket pieces needed.
Let the necessary poison move through him
as long as it can. Our ticker is not meat
and mainspring but measure and limit.

Stalwart

The wires between house and garage
could slice you as you fall, ladder a useless

set of rungs; the mailbox could
impale you, so I implore: no

roof-chores. When it's gutter time,
I stand beneath the ladder,

uncertain anchor. My father,
blond child, held his position

as ladder-bracer, even when
my grandfather threw

chunks of gutter-rot down. That's why
his hair is brown, they joke.

Your hair has darkened, too,
with gray I notice

only up close. I try to forget
the warnings from the nightly news:

melanomas and meningitis,
West Nile virus and high

triglycerides. I hold your ladder
to hold myself steady. Your sweat,

salt-heavy, drips down my cheek,
darkens my shirt. You grunt

with the effort of keeping
our house in order.

My pulse jitters every time
the ladder shifts, and I ignore

the graceful mosquito skittering
on my arm, finding purchase, digging in.

Watching the Operation

They took off your skin with a cheese slicer—
      or what seemed so, metal triangle
with a thin slit, tool crafted for paring

part from whole. I left the room.
      After the first layer, you later told me,
you looked at the widening circle,

glistening fascia over muscle, in
      a hand mirror. They went to test
the skin's edges for dissident cells.

If you could, you'd scrutinize your viscera
      or bones—curious. What's *in* there?
Husked, would we see the gray pearl

of a tumor, rosy innards, striated muscle
      hugging rib? When the lidocaine
wore off, you could feel faint tugging

but said nothing—not stoic but inquisitive,
      my empiricist who once tested stress
on engine parts. My sharp-eyed engineer.

Pronouncing the margins clear,
      they pulled your neck closed
and sewed it shut. I called the scar

your spider, black thread bristling
      at the ends, a creature I wanted
to turn away from or trap

under a glass. I dabbed on Vaseline.
        Over time, it faded—became a smile,
  or a sickle. You turned your head

in the bathroom mirror to inspect as
        the thick ridge flattened out, where once
  the irritated skin, undiagnosed,

bled small drops of purple. And,
        my head on your shoulder
  before sleep, I too watched it mend.

The Story's End

The Harlequins I read in my twenties seethed
with heat but folded closed
with a lace-gloved wedding
and gaudy honeymoon balcony sunset.
Honey, we're growing older
in the unimagined afterward. Your bones
mend slowly or not at all (pinkie
splinted for weeks, elbow slinged
from a slick February)—nothing the doctors
can do but put them in the posture of healing.
And I'm tired, my blood less red
than it should be, my stomach
divoted where the drain was sewn in,
navel rebuilt twice after laparoscopies.
In the sentimental ending to our story,
the one divined from tea leaves,
we expire simultaneously in sleep,
our bodies transforming into bees
that scatter for a new hive,
neither of us left alone to pay
the other's crematorium bill.
In medieval tales, the lovers' mortal remains
drift off toward the watery horizon
on a skiff, or blossom into honeysuckle
twined with hazel; in those romances,
the story varies infinitely. But I fear
our final pages are more prosaic,
living wills and insurance policies.
In the meantime, we'll both spit cherry pits
into the same bowl. We'll watch
romantic comedies and go to bed

at ten. As I fall asleep, I'll imagine
one possible variant ending:
In our shared afterlife, you ride
a Harley—your bucket-list steed—
into the great western hinterlands.
I write in a scented lakeside garden
while you're gone, ready with
the saga's next installment
when your motorcycle rumbles
back down the drive.

NOTES

"Preface" and "The Rules of Courtly Love (Abridged, Rev. Ed)" are indebted to the twelfth-century *De amore*, written by the cleric Andreas Capellanus of the court of Marie de Champagne. The title is often translated as *The Art of Courtly Love*, and the book purports to instruct "Walter" on the mores of courtly love.

"Paul and Fran" retells the story of Paolo and Francesca in Canto V of the *Inferno*.

"Gemma Donati in Purgatory": Gemma Donati was the wife of Dante Alighieri. As far as we can tell, she's not addressed in his poems, though there's speculation about the final word of Canto V of the Purgatorio, *gemma*, in the story of La Pia. There's no evidence for romantic love on Gemma's part: she didn't accompany Dante when he was exiled, though she later joined him in Ravenna. As Wallace Fowlie put it in his book *A Reading of Dante's* Inferno, "There is no reliable proof concerning either the happiness or unhappiness in this marriage."

"Gemma Donati, Doppiatrice": The name of Dante's wife is also the name of a woman who dubs movies in Italian, the voice of Ashley Tisdale, star of Disney's *High School Musical* and television shows. Italian *doppiatori* and *doppiatrici* often speak the voice of the same actor or actress, in whatever films they appear.

"Laura": In the 366 poems that make up Petrarch's *Canzoniere*, Laura is given voice in less than ten poems. Much of this poem is taken from her speeches and dialogue, sometimes slightly altered.

"Anne" is for Anne Boleyn.

"Him and Me" and "Eyeing a New Man": Gaspara Stampa was an Italian Renaissance writer, not widely published, who wrote a lyric sequence in the tradition of Petrarch (and was named in the *Duino Elegies* of Rilke). She was a singer of sonnets, a *virtuosa*, in Venice in the 1540s, and fell in love with Count Collaltino di Collalto, the subject of many of her poems. However (as "Eyeing a New Man" demonstrates), later poems address a second beloved, Bartolomeo Zen. She died at the age of thirty one. Though she puns on her name, *Stampa*, which connotes printing and publication in Italian, her poems were not published in her lifetime. After she died, her sister assembled a collection.

I'm indebted to Troy Tower and Jane Tylus for their edition of Stampa's *The Complete Poems* (University of Chicago Press, 2010), which readers desiring the Italian can refer to.

"Bedtime Trobairitz": The trobairitz were female troubadours. Our understanding now is that the music of troubadours sounded like plainchant. A *jongleur* is the musician who plays a troubadour's songs, and an *alba* is a dawn song, the precursor to the aubade.

"Courtly Love": Though many of the details reflect the biography of Courtney Love, I have imagined the sentiments of her and the other speakers in the sequence.

> "All You Who Hear" includes a line from Mozart's *The Marriage of Figaro*.
>
> "First Sight" uses phrases from Sir Thomas Wyatt's "Whoso List to Hunt" and "They Flee from Me."
>
> "Curt Reply" references a quote from Kurt Cobain in a 1992 *Rolling Stone* interview: "'It's like Evian water and battery acid,' Cobain says of the couple's chemistry. And when you mix the two? 'You get love,' says Cobain, smiling for the first time."

The title of "Sex, Death, Love, Hate" was part of Courtney Love's answer to a question from a Philadelphia reporter about "what fans can expect from the new album," *Died Blonde*.

"If" includes quotes from interviews with Love, only slightly altered, by Mark Yarm (*Spin*) and Nancy Jo Sales (*Vanity Fair*).

The final image of "Felicity, OH" is indebted to a picture of Felicity Woytek.

The song in "Fidelity, MO" is, of course, Journey's "Faithfully."

"Pared" is for Claudia Emerson.

"Eurydice in the ICU Waiting Room" is for Cindy Traub and John Kindschuh.

"Kant the Nephrologist": With apologies to Doctor Shashi Kant.

"Gilding the Lily": Some material courtesy of the article "Dragonflies: Strange Love," by Jennifer Ackerman, in *National Geographic*.

"Impractical Part" is for Sean Tierney.

ACKNOWLEDGMENTS

These poems appeared previously in the following journals, sometimes in a slightly different version:

32 Poems: "Needlework" and "Lady Pygmalion"; *Bear Review:* from "Courtly Love (for Courtney Love)"; *Cave Wall:* "Pared"; *Image:* "Impractical Part" and "Stalwart"; *Isthmus:* "Espoused"; *Jabberwock Review:* "Dear Lyric Address," and "Watching the Operation"; *Jet Fuel Review:* "Gemma Donati, Doppiatrice"; *Juked:* "Preface"; *Kenyon Review Online:* "Kant the Nephrologist"; *Lake Effect:* "Paul and Fran"; *Matter Monthly:* "Laura" and from "Courtly Love (for Courtney Love)"; *Mid-American Review:* "Love-Scrawls"; *Notre Dame Review:* "Pyrite"; *Pamplemousse:* "Bedtime Trobairitz"; *Poetry:* "Gilding the Lily" and "Victory, WI"; *Quiddity:* "Anne"; *Spoon River Poetry Review:* "Knight Errant"; *Unsplendid:* "Him and Me" and "Eyeing a New Man"; *Vinyl:* from "Courtly Love (for Courtney Love)"; *Waccamaw:* "Dead Ringer."

"My Weak Constitution" appeared in the anthology *Out of Sequence: The Sonnets Remixed.*

"Paul and Fran" and sections of "Courtly Love (for Courtney Love)" appeared in the anthology *The Manifesto Project.*

"Felicity, OH," "Fidelity, MO," and "Vows" appeared on the Dorothy Sargent Rosenberg Foundation website.

"The Rules of Courtly Love" was released as an eth press broadside.

Thanks to the following institutions, which provided scholarships and fellowships that enabled me to research the courtly love tradition and write some of these poems: the Institute for Advanced Catholic Studies at USC, the Sewanee Writers Conference, and the University Research Council and the Taft Family Foundation at the University of Cincinnati.

Thanks to my professors at the University of Cincinnati who helped me as I studied both courtly love and Italian: Trish Henley, Jonathan Kamholtz, Joyce Miller, Mariateresa Perrotta, and Maria Romagnoli.

Thanks to those who gave feedback on individual poems, including Brian Brodeur, George David Clark, Claudia Emerson, Tasha Golden, Linda Gregerson, Rebecca Hazelton, Troy Jollimore, Julia Koets, Dave Nielsen, Amy Ninneman, Michael C. Peterson, Linwood Rumney, Lisa Summe, Sara Watson, Ruth Williams, and my 2012 Bread Loaf and 2013 Sewanee workshop groups.

Thanks especially to those who read the full manuscript and offered advice that helped shape it, including Don Bogen, Nicole Cooley, John Drury, Ellen Elder, and Sarah Rose Nordgren.

My deepest, deepest gratitude to MK Callaway, James Long, Neal Novak, Alisa Plant, and Barbara Bourgoyne and the rest of the amazing LSU Press team for bringing this manuscript to print. Your expertise has been invaluable.

I would not have been able to revise and submit this manuscript without the childcare provided by Rose Hageman starting in 2015.

And the greatest thanks to Jeff (I hope you enjoy the imaginary motorcycle) and Jeremiah Warren.

www.ingramcontent.com/pod-product-compliance
Lightning Source LLC
Chambersburg PA
CBHW030122170426
43198CB00009B/705